THE BEAVER BOT
OF YELLOWSTONE

The Beaver Bot of Yellowstone

Pure-Play Leadership for the Artificial Intelligence Revolution

AL NAQVI AND
J. MARK MUNOZ

UNION BRIDGE BOOKS
An imprint of Wimbledon Publishing Company Limited (WPC)

UNION BRIDGE BOOKS
75–76 Blackfriars Road
London SE1 8HA

www.unionbridgebooks.com

British Library Cataloguing-in-Publication Data
A catalogue record for this book is available from the British Library.

ISBN-13: 978-1-78527-058-1 (Hbk)
ISBN-10: 1-78527-058-3 (Hbk)

This title is also available as an e-book.

*In a world characterized by robots, autonomous cars and
drones, now more than ever, our link back to nature
will be the defining factor for human civilization.*

*That is where it all began. Now, as the created become the
creators, that link will always remind us of our
genesis and who we are, who we are becoming
and who we ought to be.*

*Dedicated to the American national parks, the wildlife
and our park rangers.*

*Partial proceeds of this book will be donated
to US National Parks.*

*Many thanks to Marya for helping with
the drawings and artwork.*

CONTENTS

1 Introduction 1

2 The Story: The Great Flood and Its Aftermath 17

3 A Seeker's Search 23

4 The Rebellion 29

5 Robots and Automation—the Concept 39

6 Cognitive Capabilities 47

7 The Final Struggle 57

8 CEO Reflection 61

Questions for Review 73

Questions for Deeper Insights 75

About the Authors 77

Part Two of the Beaver Story 79

1

INTRODUCTION

As the world enters the fourth industrial revolution, you have two simple choices: lead or perish. The problem: the cognitive transformation is sweeping through the global economy, and it is not like anything traditional leaders have ever experienced before.

As retail, financial services, health care and auto sectors are discovering, the rise of intelligent automation is redefining the rules of competition. It is also changing the dynamics of leadership.

If leaders do not learn quickly, it is highly likely that their careers and their firms will perish. The intelligent automation revolution will be far more unforgiving than the Internet or the information revolution were.

There are good reasons for that prognosis.

First, nothing you have done in the past has prepared you for what lies ahead. In fact, most of your leadership skills from the past are irrelevant and inapplicable to what is needed.

Second, it is quite possible that you have not fully grasped the enormity of the cognitive revolution. You may still be trapped in the information revolution—trying to compete based on *information and process* superiority. That is not enough anymore. The new competitive advantage is "intelligent automation."

Third, your company's culture may still be recouping and recovering after the shift from the second to the third industrial revolution (i.e., transitioning to the Internet and information age) and oblivious that the fourth industrial revolution is already upon you.

Fourth, in this revolution your greatest leadership challenge will be to keep the regular business system stable, while aggressively pursuing the new pure-play leadership.

Most organizations and their leaders are lightyears behind the pure-play leaders of this new revolution. This is not just a tech revolution. It is not just an automation play. This revolution is being shaped by those who are bold, daring, ambitious and extraordinarily bright. For them, holding multiple PhDs is like owning shirts. They come from diverse fields such as neuroscience, cognitive science, computer science, mathematics, linguistics, biology, political science, public policy and others.

Some are MDs and PhDs, others engineers; and medical schooling and lifelong learning are not burdens but fun and adventure for them. Education is not meant to be a paycheck generator, but instead a vehicle for unleashing creativity to solve complex problems. Their purpose in life is not to become a monotonous cog in some corporate machine but instead to design and deploy intelligent machines that are transforming human civilization. Some are still in their 20s and others are 75-year-old professors. But what is common among them is their genius and creativity. Their work ethic is astonishing, and their sheer will to persevere under pressure immense. Most importantly, their commitment to ongoing research and openness in sharing information has propelled and shaped this revolution.

If you think you can compete with them with your traditional tech teams and workforce, think again.

If you think you can buy technology from them, forget it. They are not making the technology to sell to you. They are making the technology to automate what your firm does. They are replacing your business models with better business models.

If you think you can get your traditional consulting firms to rescue you, save yourself some big bucks and disappointment. The traditional consulting firms are now worried about their own existence and are just as perplexed as their clients.

In fact, your choices are limited. Compete and lead with the pure-play style, buy out the pure-play innovators, or wait for your near-certain demise.

However, competing with them will require you become a pure-play leader.

Walmart had limited choices. For years, the large retailer suffered from incursions by Amazon. But unlike many others who folded, Walmart decided to fight back and to do it with the pure-play style. The mighty undertaking is now showing results. Walmart realized that fighting back is not enough—it needed to be done the pure-play way. For example, other retailers, from Macy's to Nordstrom and JC Penny to Sears, thought they had chosen to fight back, but were in the game *too little, too late*. Most importantly, unlike Walmart, they were not able to mobilize the power of the pure-play leadership.

You see, pure-play leadership is different than regular leadership. It is authentic. It is all out. It is aggressive. It is bold. It is dynamic. Most importantly, it is cool.

Regardless of what you do or which sector you are in, you are now in direct competition with the AI firms. Yes, Google, Amazon and Apple are AI firms—and, yes, they will compete with you in everything from the grocery business to health care to the auto industry—but there are thousands more. These little startups—from China, the United States, Israel, Canada, India, the UK and other countries—are coming for you and your business.

Brace yourself, since in one stroke of innovation, they will replace your business model, improve and automate your core cognitive and physical processes, annihilate your economic interests and make you irrelevant.

It does not matter how big you are or how much you spend on the traditional R&D. It does not matter how large your tech departments are since this revolution is not just about information technology. It does not matter how many bright people you can hire. It does not matter how strong your supply chain is. If you do not have the fundamentals of the pure-play leadership right, you are destined to lose.

You are not ready because this is not what business schools trained you for. You are not ready because this is not what any school (even science, technology or engineering) educated you for. You were not meant to encounter the rise of machines so soon, so mightily. You were meant to operate and compete in a world with machines subservient to humans and not machines with a mind of their own. In fact, human civilization was not meant to be confronted by such a formidable force so unexpectedly. But it has happened and now you must adapt.

However, that is only half the story. The real issue is that, unlike pure-play leaders who have single-focus startups to manage, you must handle your existing business while simultaneously seeking the cognitive competitive advantage. So, while the term pure-play business may imply a single product or service-focused business, pure-play leadership is more than that.

Pure-play leadership is defined as the ability to effectively lead a firm from a traditional to a cognitive business through a systematic and disciplined effort such that the firm expands and leverages its incumbent advantage while simultaneously fostering new cognitive capabilities.

For a pure-play leader, all firms are now tech firms. They do not discriminate between tech and non-tech since they know that the competition for any business is coming not just from inside the sector, but also from the tech. Tesla is less an auto company and more a tech firm. The difference between incumbent firms and pure-play tech firms is simple. A non-tech firm asks the question: we make cars, how can we use technology to build better cars? A pure-play tech firms asks the question: we are a tech firm; how can we make cars?

Imitating the pure-play style is not enough. Since pure-play is about authenticity, the saying "fake it till you make it" does not work. It is a different frame of mind. It is not about wearing jeans or sandals to work or having earrings or long hair. It is also not about being a tech genius. It is not about placing ping-pong tables in workplaces and giving employees free soda. It is about authentic pure-play leadership.

One of the present authors had the opportunity to visit the headquarters of a major retailer in Chicago. Once a legendary brand name, this retailer has struggled to stay alive. Tired of failing, the leadership decided to emulate Amazon's strategy. So, they hired a large tech team, opened offices in India and attempted to act like a tech firm. They placed ping-pong and pool tables for employees and tried to act all techy.

But their culture and capabilities were not genuinely pure-play. It was phony, and all those things seemed pretentious. It was like a gazelle trying to act like a leopard. There was no authenticity. The company's culture was infested with turf battles, old-style managers pursuing politics, backbiting and power plays. One could see that despite all the entertainment contraptions, employees seemed fearful, demotivated and depressed. Key talent brought in from the high-tech firms left. Not surprisingly, the retailer continues to be on life support.

The same author also studied one of the world's largest financial companies that specialized in the mortgage industry. Situated in Northern Virginia, this firm also attempted to act like a tech firm. It hired tons of tech talent and thought that it had become a tech firm. Ironically, despite claiming to be a tech firm, the firm only promoted people from business backgrounds to senior positions. What ensued was the same old drama, political games, posturing and silos. In fact, hiring all the IT talent had the opposite effect. Every VP and director began launching his or her own pet projects. Without any coordinated tech strategy, plan or vision, in a matter of few years a complex spaghetti of systems appeared. Then the firm had to hire external consultants just so they could take an inventory of thousands of systems and figure out how they were linked to each other. All this while the firm suffered heavy losses and was eventually placed in conservatorship.

Clearly, leaders of traditional businesses need to develop pure-play leadership traits and styles. Our objective is to teach you the basics. But we want to do it with a fable. We believe that the lessons learned in the story we are about to tell you will be transformational and memorable.

While our story could have transpired in the realm of intelligent machines and artificial intelligence labs, we want to take you to the greatest pure-play lab of all: Nature.

Nature is a great teacher. It offers a solutions lab that has perfected its answers with millions of years of experimentation and optimization.

As humans appeared on the canvas of this planet, the first cognitive revolution took shape in this lab. As we prepare for the second cognitive revolution, we need to seek lessons from the first. Wisdom that is as basic as rocks and trees, as mountains and creeks, as trails and lakes will guide you to learn the most powerful lessons. The wisdom of the universe is embedded in nature. Here is the story that will stay with you and teach you the basics of pure-play leadership.

Cognitive Competition: The CEO Challenge

It all began when three strangers serendipitously discovered a lost treasure of ancient wisdom.

It was pure fate, chance or luck—but it was the best thing that happened to these individuals, and it happened when they least expected it.

All of them had felt this awkward pressure, but none of them could place a finger on why.

None of them went out searching for the solution to the problem they knew little about, but each could sense that it existed. In fact, they did not even know where to begin.

They were attendees at a conference in Wyoming's Yellowstone area. Other than that, the only thing common among them was that they were the CEOs of major companies. Henry was the CEO of an auto giant, Nancy was the CEO of a health care/pharma system and Bob was the CEO of a large retailer.

In one of the exercises at the conference, executives were required to network and share business problems and issues with one another. They were divided into teams of three and then sent to different parts of the Grand Teton and Yellowstone Park areas—and there they were expected to reflect upon their key issues and opportunities. Nancy,

Henry and Bob ended up being on the same team. Each team was assigned a facilitator.

It was in the early morning hours when Dennis, their guide and facilitator, picked them up at the front entrance of the hotel. He was driving a Ford truck. It was so early that families with children were still fast asleep in their hotel rooms. A whole day of activities in the Yellowstone and Grand Teton parks is almost as tiring as a day spent at Disney World.

As the three executives hopped into Dennis's truck, they were quiet, distant and reserved. But that was about to change.

Dennis was pleasant, cheerful and seemed very welcoming. He introduced himself and asked the others to introduce themselves. Soon, it was as if they had known him all their lives.

The sun rose, and light spread over the mountains. They stopped to grab some coffee and breakfast sandwiches, then drove north toward Yellowstone Park.

"So where are we heading and what's on the agenda?" Nancy asked. She was sitting in the front passenger seat.

"We will be spending the day in the Yellowstone Park area," Dennis replied. There was this friendly style in Dennis's speech—as if he had to fight saying, "dude," at the end of his sentences. "There is no agenda. The agenda is developed based on what's on your mind. I take you to where you need to be."

That was an awkward answer. The executives exchanged glances.

"What do you mean, Dennis?" Henry asked.

"It means dealing with the biggest thing on your mind. You see, Yellowstone is not just a park, it is a source of inspiration and life lessons. It powers the soul and the spirit. You can find solutions to your greatest business problems by reflecting upon the lessons from the park. Why don't we start with you Henry? What's on your mind? What's your big business problem today?"

"Okay!" Henry paused, clenched his lips, raised his eyebrows and could not help but say, as if he were protesting, "You mean you want me to discuss my business problem here in the truck?"

"Absolutely," Dennis replied with a smile as he looked at him in the rearview mirror. Their eyes met, and Henry felt a sense of comfort.

"Okay." Henry surrendered and proceeded. "I guess it is about the rise of autonomous cars. These cars have suddenly popped up, and the auto sector is finding itself unprepared. We focused so much on the mechanical and electrical side of our cars that we didn't develop those capabilities. We thought they were way in the future, but they seem to be coming out fast."

"That's a great answer, Henry. Thank you. Bob, how about you?" Dennis intended to get the conversation going.

"Hmm, I guess I'd have to say that my biggest concern is the rapid rise of Amazon. Amazon is taking our business left and right. We had to shut down hundreds of stores across the country." Bob's voice was monotone, as if he were sleep-talking. "We tried to emulate their technology and business model, but even though our online presence has all the bells and whistles, we seem to be missing something. Consumers are just not responding to us as they do to Amazon. Amazon keeps developing superior technology and expanding its presence in different areas. Seems like we stand no chance against them."

"We are making progress. Thank you, Bob."

Dennis then pointed to an elk that was standing on the roadside. This early there were only a few cars. Any other time and there would have been a traffic jam with tourists trying to take pictures of the wildlife. Bob, Nancy and Henry pulled out their smart phones and began to photograph the elk.

"How about you, Nancy?" Dennis asked.

Nancy smiled and said "I think my biggest problem is trying to understand how to use all that data we have accumulated for years. My firm has two sides—we are a hospital system and we also own a pharmaceutical company. We have so much data—clinical data, preclinical data, claims data—that we don't even know where to begin. With the upcoming personalized medicine and advances in genomics, we are entering a new phase of health care."

"Awesome! This is all the information I needed to take you where Yellowstone can provide answers to your questions," Dennis said this with a big smile. "You've all described your greatest business challenges. Now, here's a question for you. Your issues seem to have a common denominator. Do you know what it is?"

The CEOs exchanged puzzled glances.

Nancy volunteered: "Is it the information revolution?"

"No," Dennis responded. "Actually, the information revolution is over, and a new revolution has begun. You see, the information transformation began thousands of years ago, when a human drew a figure in a cave. The problem with that figure was that it couldn't be shared unless other humans were in the cave, too.

"Then humans developed writing, which meant that information could be passed from one party to another party. It was still inadequate since it could only be shared with a limited number of parties. Then, came printing, where information could be shared from one to many. And then came the Internet, where information can be shared from many to many. But just as a train can go only as far as its tracks, this is the maturity point of the information revolution. We have now entered the cognitive revolution—a new era has begun.

"The problem of autonomous car competition for Henry; the competitive challenge from smarter and more advanced Amazon bots for Bob; and the opportunity to revolutionize health care for Nancy—they all have a single common denominator, a key word. That key word is AIR," Dennis grinned.

"Air—as in the air we breathe?" Nancy asked, eyebrows raised.

Henry added, "Or air as in the hot air balloon?" There was a little tone of sarcasm in his question.

Dennis laughed. "Breathe in lots of air here. It's clean, the top-grade air in the world—a blessing of our national parks. But, no, AIR as in Artificial Intelligence and Robotics. Your businesses have changed. The surrounding conditions and environments have changed. In fact, I can tell you something very important: you have entered the Cognitive Competition era. You are no longer in the information age."

"Cognitive competition?" Bob asked. "What's that? I've never heard of that before."

"Yep. That's the root cause of your worries. That's why all of you are puzzled and stressed. Things are happening all around you, but no one has clarified this for you. No one has explained what is transpiring. No one has given you the tools to effectively compete in the cognitive era. You still function as if you are in the information era. When the Internet gained popularity many companies continued to do things the way they were doing prior to the Internet revolution. They were wiped out. Those who fail to understand the significance of the cognitive revolution stand no chance. The answer to your concerns lies in Yellowstone Park."

Bob and Nancy were intrigued. They could sense that Dennis had something up his sleeve. But Henry was still a little anxious and skeptical. He leaned forward, folded and placed his arms on the back of Dennis's seat.

"You'd have to explain a little more," Henry said. "I'm still puzzled."

Dennis replied: "The thing is that there are many executives who attend our conferences, and I talk to many of them. Lately, all of them have been affected by only one thing: Intelligent Automation. Unfortunately, many don't realize what they're tackling or confronted with. Some just call it technology, others call it data science, but it appears they don't understand the frameworks and the models behind the cognitive revolution. They lack the fundamental domain knowledge behind cognitive competition. That knowledge hasn't been codified or disseminated. It hasn't been formalized, and executives are approaching solutions tactically, sometimes even with brute force. Just like anything else, cognitive competition, too, requires a strategy. You see, a cognitive business is the one that derives its competitive advantage via intelligent automation."

Dennis slowed down his truck and turned onto a dirt road as he continued: "So, we posed the question to Yellowstone, and the park gave us an answer. In fact, we discovered a powerful story that took place here in Yellowstone."

Dennis next made a right turn, passed through thick bushes, and stopped the truck. As the others looked up, a breathtaking scene suddenly appeared, and everyone gasped with admiration. A cool blue creek flowed few feet from where they were parked. Beyond the creek were lush green prairies. Herds of buffalo grazed as picturesque mountains rose and touched the clouds in the back.

They all stepped out of the truck, and Dennis led them to a nearby picnic table. The magnificence of the moment mesmerized them, and for a little while no one said a thing. It was as if their souls had merged with the valley, and all became one and the same.

They had their coffee cups and breakfast sandwiches with them as they sat around the picnic table. They noticed a beaver dam in the creek. Two beavers were busy at work building the dam. The table was laid out such that all had the view of the valley. The calmness of the surroundings gave them inner strength and clarity. A sense of serenity opened their minds to imagination and new experience. And that was when Dennis told them the beaver story.

Pure-Play Leadership Lessons

Lesson 1: All firms are now tech firms and should be led as such. A cognitive business is a business that derives its competitive advantage via intelligent automation. The cognitive revolution (also known as the fourth revolution, the intelligent automation revolution and the artificial intelligence revolution) has begun. In this revolution, data is used to teach machines to make decisions and predictions. With machine learning, machines can become intelligent. You can have intelligent software machines (software bots or robots), and you can have intelligent physical machines (robots).

Lesson 2: Pure-play leadership is the ability to effectively lead a firm from a traditional to a cognitive business through a systematic and disciplined effort such that the firm expands and leverages its incumbent advantage while simultaneously fostering new cognitive capabilities.

Lesson 3: The traditional barriers to entry are no longer valid. Competition can come from anywhere.

Lesson 4: Authenticity is key to being a pure-play leader. Faking will not work.

Lesson 5: Pretending to be a tech culture is futile. Employees will see right through it, and the traditional turf wars and destructive politics will not end.

2

THE STORY: THE GREAT FLOOD AND ITS AFTERMATH

A long time ago, there lived a civilization of beaver people in the area we now call Yellowstone Park. Of course, they had no way of knowing that it would someday become a park, so they only called it Yellowstone. The beaver people were intelligent, adventurous and enterprising.

Grasslands spread under the shadows of tall and proud mountains; clouds rubbed shoulders with the peaks and saw their reflection glide over the foothills, into the flower filled prairies and then drift over the carefree swiveling creek where water flowed obsessively and splashed madly against the rocks. The creek snaked through the valley like a dormant whip holding the ultimate power to shape the destiny of the valley.

Somewhere across the tallest peak, where the creek bent sharply and abruptly, the ferocity of raging water suddenly died down. As if tamed by the touch of an angel, the calm of a pond appeared, creating a zone of tranquility. A break from the wild waters that flowed before and after it, the pond paradise was not only the home for, but also the creation of, the beaver people.

Round the clock, they had worked for years to ensure this refuge would stay serene and safe, and its peace would attract many other life-forms.

Workers they were—resilient and always committed. Beavers got their inspiration from what they created.

The beaver society was divided into five major groups.

The first group was known as Producers. All Producers carried hammers, chisels, axes and saws. They built dams and collected food for all members of the beaver colony.

The second group was known as Engineers. They made hammers, chisels, axes and saws used by the Producers.

The third group was known as Consultants and they were the advisors to all other groups.

The fourth group was known as Information Beavers who focused on creating, processing, and managing information to ensure that the beaver people knew the best and safest places to find trees, shrubs and rocks.

The fifth group was known as the Governing group. This group led the beaver colony and made decisions that impacted all others.

Each morning, the Producer beavers took their hammers, chisels, axes and saws, and carefully scraped off tree bark. The bark provided nutritious food for the entire beaver colony. After beavers scraped and skirted a tree, they would then gently push and make it fall. The fallen tree was carefully sliced into smaller pieces, and branches and logs were transported back to the creek to build dams and lodges where all beavers lived.

The beaver colony was led by a leader who above all else cherished wisdom. "Progress can neither be denied nor controlled," he would say to the beaver people. "Yet it must be approached responsibly." His name was simply Beaver Leader.

Most beavers respected and admired Beaver Leader, and he loved the beavers. Some beavers of the Governing group did not like Beaver Leader but accepted him as the rightful leader of the group.

But on an afternoon in the early months of the Beaver Calendar, Beaver Leader faced the greatest challenge of his leadership. Something unexpected had happened. Some beavers had anticipated this coming but most, including Beaver Leader, did not expect it to happen so suddenly and with such ferocity. Now, it had turned into a matter of life and death.

Beaver Leader remembered the good old days when life was fun, and rapid change was rare. Those were the days when Engineers and Consultants would come up with innovative ideas on how to manufacture better hammers, chisels, axes and saws.

"Producers will be able to scrape off barks faster and easier and you can sell more tools," the Consultant told the Engineers. It did not take Engineers long to get busy to make new hammers, chisels, axes and saws—and for Producers to start using them.

Producers were ecstatic. For centuries, they had used hammers, chisels, axes and saws and had never once thought about how to make better tools. But now they had more advanced tools. Their hammers, chisels, axes and saws were mechanical and powerful.

Time moved on and beaver people became very good at scraping off bark and felling trees. They were making lodges and dams faster, and the quality of their dams and lodges was far superior than before.

Plenty of food was available. Beavers thrived and so did their pond, which became the prime attraction for many types of life-forms, including moose, elk, deer, and buffalo. Birds made nests and spent their spring and summers there. Turtles and fish found refuge. Even predators such as wolves, coyotes and grizzlies occasionally visited— though they were not really welcomed. As the pond hosted a broad variety of life, everyone respected and admired beavers for their skills and hard work.

With the new tools and their effective use, the overall performance increased. Year after year, the size, safety and quality of the pond improved.

Information beavers enhanced their skills to search, identify and locate new trees and stones. They created maps and developed faster and better mechanisms to supply and distribute trees, branches, and rocks. Consultants and Information beavers worked together and constantly improved the logistics and supply operations.

As time passed, and Producers began working increasingly farther away from the banks of the creek, Information beavers established a complex communication system known as the Beaver Screamer. The Beaver Screamer connected all beavers such that every one of them could pass information to every other member of the beaver colony.

This made them more advanced and led to even higher productivity increase.

But then that something unexpected happened. Such things tend to happen when systems become complex and unstable.

One year, the snowfall was excessive, and spring arrived early and the climate heated faster than any beaver had expected. Snow melted quickly and unleashed a never-before-seen-flood that gushed through the creek and destroyed everything in its path. The beaver people stood on the banks, helpless and shocked, and watched in horror as the floodwaters washed away their dam. Years of work gone in a split second.

When birds returned from their winter refuge, there was no pond left. They flew down the creek to look for logs and branches that the water had taken downstream but could find none and reported that finding back to the distraught beaver people.

The moose and the elk and the deer and the buffalo came to pay their respects and commiserate with the beavers. Most visitors simply shook their heads in disbelief. Some gave hugs and solemnly promised that they would never abandon the beaver people. But deep inside they knew that with the pond gone, it would be hard for them to stay in the area. Need, in most cases, drives desperate action and it can often endorse personal interest over social interest.

Pure-Play Leadership Lessons

Lesson 6: Pure-play leaders recognize that successful pure-play leadership be will the greatest test of their leadership and careers (refer to the definition of pure-play leadership).

Additional Explanation: The nature of competition is about to change. Embracing the cognitive revolution and managing during these highly uncertain times will be the true test of leadership. Companies and business processes will have to be reinvented. Skills and capabilities that were once thought of as belonging exclusively to the tech firms will now be needed in all firms. As leaders brace for this great transformation, they must realize that it will be the greatest challenge of their careers, and when they succeed and look back, nothing will look the same. A great renewal is taking shape.

A SEEKER'S SEARCH

Situational assessment was necessary. Consultants analyzed the situation and determined the beavers people would need to work harder and faster to recover. They made their report, and it came as a shock to everyone that five years of work would need to be done in one work year.

But there was an added complexity to the problem. Information beavers reported that the productivity enhancements of the past had enabled the beavers to remove an excessive number of trees from the area surrounding the pond. This implied that to get new trees, beaver teams would have to wander farther out into the forest. This meant they would have to explore new areas of forest and then cut and drag trees back to the creek from far away. That would involve not only extra work, but also tremendously higher risk. Bears, coyotes, and wolves may have behaved relatively well when they visited the pond but when beavers would be far out into the territory of bear, coyote and wolf, all bets were off. Undoubtedly, the wilderness instincts of the predators would become more dominant than their social skills.

In addition to safety and productivity issues, beavers had to think about the social pressure they faced. If they did not build the dam fast enough, birds and animals would start leaving and move elsewhere. Their eco-system would be destroyed. The beaver people would no longer be admired and viewed as contributors to the society.

In other words, their way of life would be over.

Whenever Beaver Leader was confronted with major problems, he would walk down to the hot spring area. This was something he had learned from his late father, and his father had learned this from his ancestors. Now known as Old Faithful, in those days it was a nameless geyser that shot up water every few beaver hours. Beaver Leader loved watching the geyser shoot up in boiling water, hearing the gurgling and splashing sounds it made, seeing the steam and vapors rise, and even smelling the pungent smell of sulfur.

"There are two lessons to learn here, Shorty," his father once said. "First let your feelings out as this geyser lets water out. No point in keeping them internalized. Be honest with yourself. Bring things out to the surface. Second, learn from this geyser the virtue of being dependable. It always comes through every few beaver hours and that is why it is fun watching it. If I were to give a name to this geyser it would be Dependable," his father said.

When he arrived at the geyser, Beaver Leader found a rock and sat there waiting for the geyser to erupt as he pondered his problem.

If he did not rebuild a new dam at the current place, he would have to lead the beaver people out to a new location. It might take years to find one. There is a risk that they may never find a new spot or, worse, become food for wolves and bears before they find one. The thought made him shudder.

Even if he made his people work harder, they may not be able to accomplish five years' worth of work in one year. Most likely they would not finish the work, and winter would arrive. He knew that, if unprepared, he would risk losing more than half of his beaver people in the harsh winter months. In fact, if things become worse, none might survive.

He looked at the rock he was sitting on and smiled as he loudly said the phrase "talk about being caught between a rock and a hard place." This self-humor reduced his stress a bit.

It appeared that there were no feasible solutions.

As he thought about his problem, the afternoon turned into evening, and the evening turned into night. He did not move. Clouds came, rain fell, stars shone and then disappeared, light gently parted from the darkness and then sun rose. If he had been counting, he would have known the geyser had erupted at least nine times while he was there. A patch of cloud came from somewhere and, after a feeble attempt to make rain, passed on. Winds stayed calm, and sunshine gleamed over the geyser area. Sun rose higher as Beaver Leader's hopes waned.

Broken and still without a solution, he realized he needed some food and water. He jumped from the rock and headed to a nearby wooded area. He found a small puddle of rainwater. After checking the water's temperature, he took a quick dive. Then he found an aspen tree and began to gnaw and chew the bark. His body needed nutrition, and this was his favorite food. As he was busy eating, he saw another tree, which was situated right across the aspen. It was a lodgepole pine.

Beaver Leader vividly remembered the first time he tasted the pine bark. He hated the taste. He was with his father. His dad took the first bite and pushed him forward to try it. When he spit it out, his dad laughed: "Shorty, I know you're not going to love the taste of the fresh bark from this tree but this tree is more than food. It is a teacher. Do remember the lesson from lodgepole pines. They are resilient. Their power lies in their ability to grow roots in very thin soil. Be a lodgepole pine Shorty [...] be a lodgepole. When the soil gets thin, figure out a way to grow roots horizontally. Fight back. When things become tough, fight hard. There is always a solution."

"Ok, Dad," he responded sincerely and respectfully. "I will remember the lesson."

"That's not the only lesson, Shorty. Lodgepole pines are not too flashy or flamboyant. They stay humble, and other trees often grow taller and cover them. But when lightning strikes and all trees burn down—including the lodgepoles—you know what happens? Their cones fall on the ground and those are tough cones to crack. The heat from the fire cracks the cones and seeds come out and new trees grow from the seeds. Amazingly, the forest survives. That is renewal, son. Remember, when you face the toughest challenge of your life – that's when your renewal happens. That's when you become a true leader. Those are the defining times, Shorty. When the game gets unwinnable, change the rules of the game. Be a lodgepole," his dad said.

He remembered the exact words of his dad, as he heard them over and over again in his mind.

"Be a lodgepole." Beaver Leader stopped chewing and whispered to himself, "When the game becomes unwinnable, change the rules of the game."

"When the game becomes unwinnable, change the rules of the game," he repeated.

And that was the moment when Beaver Leader figured out the solution to his problems. It seemed way out there, in some ways impossible—but it was a solution. It was worth trying. He needed the counsel of his team.

Pure-Play Leadership Lessons

Lesson 7: Denial is not an option. The fourth industrial revolution has arrived and there is no option but to respond. Clear thinking and a calm courageous demeanor will be essential. Bold vision, risk taking, and out of the box thinking will be necessary.

Additional Explanation: Unlike the twentieth century's competitive models, the cognitive revolution is neither about simple automation, nor about information processing. It is about "intelligence". It is based upon "intelligent work automation". Intelligent machines, both digital and physical, will be the source of value and competitive advantage. This strategy needs to be at the center of all business planning.

THE REBELLION

Beaver Leader rushed back and demanded the beaver people assemble for an emergency meeting.

When all the beavers had assembled, even the beaver children, he said, "We are all good beavers. So many life-forms depend upon us. We are hard-working, enterprising and productive beavers. As we became more efficient, we built a bigger and better pond. That pond supported us and many other life-forms. But then the unfortunate event happened. The flood wiped it all out. Today, we face our greatest challenge. Consultants and Engineers are telling us that we would need to do five years of work in one work year. We had already used all the trees that were close to the banks of our creek. The trees farther away are in reach but will require tremendously hard work, and it will be extremely risky to send the working teams out there. This is the toughest challenge we have ever faced. Plain and simple, it is the choice between doing something drastic or we face extinction. But we are the beaver people. Nothing is impossible for us and we are used to doing drastic things. As my father used to say, when the game becomes unwinnable, change the rules of the game. Today, I can feel his presence among us. Another lesson he taught me was to do what the lodgepole does. It finds the power to renew itself when it faces its most threatening challenge. We will renew and reinvent ourselves—just as the lodgepole does. We will let our cones burn down so we can crack them and allow new seeds to spill." He delivered a powerful speech and, after a brief pause, said, "We will create a beaver robot. This robot will do the work for us. This bot will cut and fetch the trees for us." As soon as Beaver Leader said those words, the assembly participants gasped, and there was an uncomfortable silence.

Some thought that the Beaver Leader has lost his mind. "Finally, that sulfur got to his head," whispered a young female beaver to her friends, and they giggled.

But many Information Beavers and Consultants took his comments seriously. The head of the Information group, Ken, raised his hand and, when Beaver Leader authorized him to talk, said, "Beaver Leader, I think what you have said is completely doable. In fact, now that I think about it, this is probably the only viable opportunity we have.

I have been researching this field for years. I think it can be done. It will need a different line of thinking, but it can be done."

"I disagree," Caesar, a Governing beaver, said forcefully. "I think we need to do what our core competency is. We can develop better information about where the trees are, improve our supply chain, and beef up our work to create a new dam."

"Have you not seen the report?" Ken asked Caesar. "There is no way we can finish it before the winter arrives."

"Who is to say that we can finish creating what Leader is saying," Caesar persisted. "Our best chance is to do what we know best and do it better than ever. There is no need to introduce this extraordinary complexity of developing robots to do our work."

The lead engineer, Sarah, said, "Look the strategy to do both—survive and achieve the ultimate capability of having an automated workforce—can only help us."

Oliver, the head of Consulting chimed in: "Look, you guys and gals, both Engineers and Information beavers are scientists, and you want to create things for pleasure. I get that. But you should not be setting the strategy." He pointed toward Sarah and continued. "Your work belongs in your labs. Strategy belongs with us and the Governing group."

"Actually, strategy doesn't just belong with you," Sarah replied confidently. "I am not sure you are fully grasping what is transpiring here. We are changing the nature of work. We are creating a smart digital and robotic work-force. The strategy belongs with all of us, the scientists and engineers and all other groups. We can create an entire beaver bot workforce that will dramatically shift the odds in our favor. While you will still be figuring out your strategy models and developing pointless and fancy presentations, we would have changed the future of the beaver civilization. We can no longer discriminate based upon who is entitled to run strategy and who is not. That is such an antiquated approach to conduct our affairs."

Sarah seemed annoyed by being viewed as someone who would not know what strategy is simply because she was a scientist.

"That is not strategy, Caesar said disapprovingly. "That is just technology. It is fanciful thinking." He appeared angry.

"Technology is the strategy," Sarah replied. "What are you missing here? If it is fanciful thinking, then so be it. At least we would try to create a bold future rather than being trapped in an antiquated mindset and some fancy presentations."

Oliver jumped into the conversation again: "Yes, but what Beaver Leader is saying means that we would need to do two things simultaneously. It is hard enough to do one. Making dams and lodges, and finding food, are major undertakings. Now Beaver Leader wants to add making robots and digital workforce. That adds a whole new dimension of complexity. I am not sure we can do that. If anything, we should do what we have always done. Let us simply improve our processes without introducing the added complexity. The incumbent model is working."

Sarah was not going to give up. "What if there is another flood? In fact, I think we should have done this automation a long time ago. The incumbent model is working but to what end. If we fail to make the dam, and the winter begins, we will be gone – all of us. Not a single beaver will survive."

"Frankly, folks, if we cannot see things eye to eye, we must split," Caesar said angrily. "Those who desire to experiment with this fabricated and concocted story can take their chances. Others can follow me. I am going to build a dam downstream, and I am going to do it the old way."

Before Beaver Leader got a chance to intervene, the hot-tempered Caesar got up and starting walking out of the assembly. But what disappointed Beaver Leader most was that nearly four out of five beavers followed Caesar. What began as a full assembly was now nearly deserted. Only few remained. Tension was high as in some cases members of the same family made different decisions. Anxiety mounted, and anger was in the air. They had just lost their homes and the dam, and now they were about to lose each other.

As Caesar and his followers prepared to depart, Beaver Leader knew he could not stop them. They had made up their minds.

"Just remember, you will always have a place here," Beaver Leader said as he wiped tears from his eyes. "You will always be welcome back here."

Caesar did not answer and walked away into the darkness, followed by a large procession carrying tools, food, and belongings.

Beaver Leader quickly surveyed who remained. Much to his relief, those who stayed were from all groups and backgrounds. He knew that he would need a diverse set of skills to be successful.

One member of the Consultant group raised her hand and said, "I have been researching about artificial intelligence and robotics. I believe in you, Beaver Leader. I am willing to give this project everything. If we are going to die, we are going to die trying for something big." She adjusted her eyeglasses and wiped her tears.

"Beaver Leader, I can help in developing this also," a Producer member shouted. "I know the processes that can be performed by the robot."

A young Consultant raised his hand and showed his commitment to Beaver Leader's vision. "You know, as Consultants we're always coming up with nice names and acronyms. Can we give a name to the beaver robot and call it the Beaver Bot of Yellowstone?" Everyone in the assembly hall burst into laughter. Laughter helped them cope with the intense pain they were experiencing.

"So be it. It will be known as the Beaver Bot of Yellowstone," said Beaver Leader.

After a pause, he continued: "Okay, I am happy to hear that all of you who remained are ready to face the challenge. Let this be the day when we all decided that we will reinvent ourselves. This is the day, when we will launch this project to make a beaver robot—sorry, to make the Beaver Bot of Yellowstone." Beaver Leader smiled and looked in the direction of the Consultant who had thought up the name. "I am authorizing the deployment of a team to accomplish this project. We will divert our resources and apply the full strength of our powerful talent. Sarah will lead this project with me. We will form a project team that will be from all five groups. We will also deploy another team that will ensure that we continue to meet our daily essential survival needs. But we will all be a united powerful team with the collective single mission to save our civilization from an existential threat. In this endeavor, there will be no silos, no ranks, no predetermined bias toward anyone. We are all part of the strategy and we are all part of the execution. We will all hold each other accountable. Folks, this is our first plan, and this is our backup plan. We have five months to complete this before the winter begins. We were good at building dams and now we must become good at building bots that build good dams. These are the defining times for us. Let's make it happen."

There was loud cheering, and Beaver Leader received a standing ovation.

Pure-Play Leadership Lessons

Lesson 8: Be decisive. Pure-play leaders are decisive. Once they decide, they are quick to implement.

Lesson 9: Speed of execution is essential. Do not wait. Act fast. Drive results. Pure-play leaders understand that timing is everything.

Lesson 10: Relentless pressure. Get used to extremely aggressive deadlines. Learn to deal with the immense pressure. Work becomes constant, and it may feel like nothing exists except work. But that is the only way extraordinary results are achieved.

Lesson 11: "Wow" product and service focus. Pure-play leaders have no time for petty politics. Their leadership is authentic and focused on only one thing: improving the future with a "wow" product or service that truly add value for consumers.

Lesson 12: The cool factor. Pure-play leaders love to pursue the challenge of delivering "wow" products and services. For them cool is not about their own selves, but instead is about creating the ecosystem that works together to create the "wow" factor. It is not their persona but the integrated ecosystem that becomes cool. This products and services, processes, people, culture, brands—everything transforms into cool.

Lesson 13: Destroy elitism. Pure-play leaders do not create silos or caste systems between who are "strategic" people and who are not. This is one of the biggest factors that separates the non-pure-play versus pure-play leaders. Traditional leaders, often a product of the antiquated management and leadership training system, view that only some are entitled to influence strategy. Typically, former consultants from major strategy firms, MBAs from Ivy League universities, or people from certain backgrounds are viewed as "strategic," while scientists and engineers are often awarded the status of "technically sound but non-strategic." This classification is ridiculous in the modern world and has no merit. Pure-play leaders know that as the world moves forward, the soft skills once considered necessary for the corporate world will be replaced by hard technical skills. And it is much easier for the tech geeks to understand business than it is for MBAs to understand technology.

Lesson 14: Truth is power. Rational and data-driven decision making is key. Ambition is always nurtured and guided by rationality and a data-driven search for truth.

Lesson 15: All held accountable by all. Pure-play leaders make sure systems are implemented that hold all accountable by all. This means a new type of organizational team dynamic develops where authority is not top-down but emerges through a collective commitment to accomplish great things.

Lesson 16: Dual Leadership. Implies leaders identify the core competence of their firm and then extrapolate it to the tech level. For example, we are good in making drugs, and now we must become good in making technology that discovers and makes new medicines.

5

ROBOTS AND AUTOMATION—THE CONCEPT

The following day a guidance council and a project team were created, and the project team was immediately deployed. The team found a nearby cave and called it the "War Room." Beaver Leader kicked off the team meeting and began by developing the theoretical concepts behind the project.

"Since this is an important project for us and it will provide guidance for our future projects, let me write down the key lessons." Beaver Leader said and proceeded to a side wall and wrote the following:

- Decide on renewal. Make an executive decision to reinvent and redefine yourself.
- Understand that this journey means building dual competencies in both dam building and bot building.
- Lead the cultural transformation to create unparalleled innovation.
- Organize a cross-functional team to launch a major effort.

"My dad once quoted someone who said, 'give me six hours to chop down a tree and I will spend the first four sharpening the axe'—the first thing we need to do is to develop some high-level theory and plan. So, who wants to go first?"

Sarah volunteered to go first. "We are developing a beaver robot. A beaver robot has two sides to it. It has the cognitive side and it has a physical side. There are things for which it will have to use its cognitive skills, there are things for which it will have to use its physical capabilities, and then there are things in which it would have to use both." She took a stick and made several diagrams on the wall of the cave.

Cognitive work zone Analyzing, thinking, deciding	**Physical & cognitive work zone** Physical robot with intelligent actions	

Virtual work zone Human-controlled software	**Physical work zone** Non-autonomous robot moving, dexterity, balancing, strength	

High — Cognitive capability — Low

Low — **Physical capability** — High

Workforce intelligent automation

	Virtual	Physical
High	Autonomous bots	Autonomous robots
	Robotic process automation	Semiautonomous robots
Low	Regular software	Robots

Intelligence

Modality

"We can visualize the beaver robot capabilities on two dimensions: cognitive and physical. Certain physical attributes of the artifact we are building would require advanced physical capabilities such as motion, dexterity, physical strength, power, balance and so forth. On the other end, it would need cognitive capabilities including things such as analyzing, thinking, decision-making and so forth. Then we can have the area where we will integrate the two capabilities to realize the combined power of electromechanical and cognitive components," Sarah said.

"What about the four quadrants?" a Consultant asked.

"Good question. Each quadrant represents something unique. For a long time, we have made improvements in both software and physical domains. For example, we made better axes, better saws, better hammers and better chisels. But our tools were not intelligent or smart. They were simply more powerful or more automated or more efficient. Because we improved our information-processing capabilities, now we can move our digital or virtual products, communications, as well as physical tools upwards to become more intelligent. Intelligence can be added to both software and robots. Note that low intelligence process automation software is known as Robotic Process Automation—even though it is software and not a robot. This means our quadrant can be divided into four areas. Upper right is smart robotics and includes robots that can function autonomously. Lower right is non-autonomous robotics. Lower left is software, upper left is autonomous agent software. The middle part on the left side is robotic process automation. Robotic process automation means digital automation of clerical and data entry type processes." Sarah paused for a moment. "Now it is incumbent upon us to identify all the processes and desired products or services that we want to produce that fall into these categories."

"PC-Square," one of the Consultants uttered.

"What's that?" Sarah inquired.

"Forgive me for being a consultant and as you know we always come up with fancy names. Let me give this model a name. P stands for physical capabilities, C stands for cognitive, and Square implies the upwards movement for both software and physical robots."

Everyone smiled as they heard the Consultant beaver come up with yet another fancy name. "All right then, from now on this model will be known as the PC-Square model," Sarah said then resumed her analysis. "Please note that what we are doing here is workforce intelligent automation, and that means both software and robots need to be made intelligent. In our case, for example, we are making a beaver robot and it would need the following cognitive skills: sensing, analyzing, deciding, searching, seeking, reasoning and so forth. For instance, it would need to know the difference between various trees, discriminate between things that are obstacles and things that are not, figure out the best way to cut the tree, and make decisions related to which tree to cut. It will also need the capabilities to move around, to cut a tree, to chop, to scrape a bark, to cut the branches, and the capability to carry the resources back to the creek. Finally, when combined it would need to understand how to move around, avoid obstacles while moving around, how and when to cut a tree it has decided to cut, figure out the best way to transport trees back, and how to use the tools." Sarah proceeded to draw this on the cave wall:

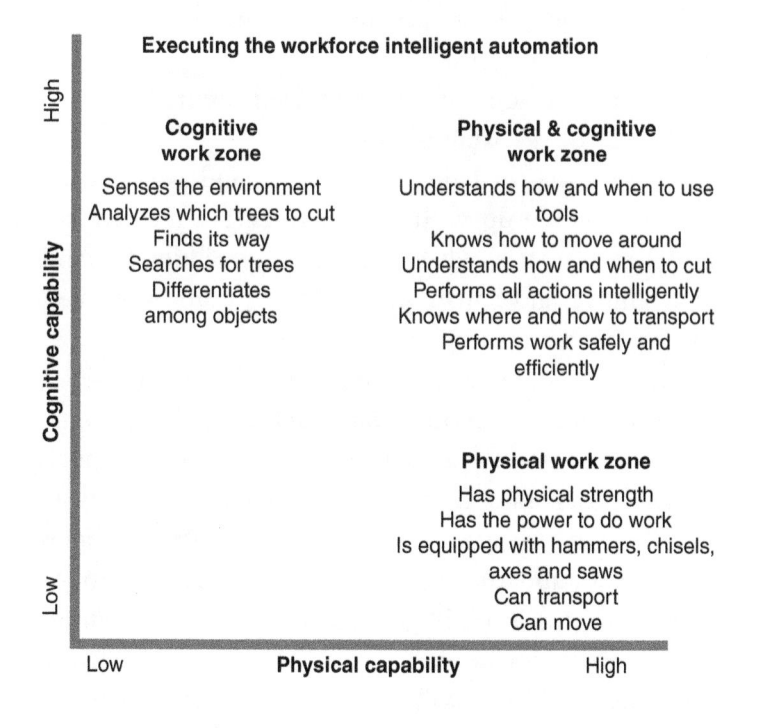

Executing the workforce intelligent automation

Cognitive work zone
Senses the environment
Analyzes which trees to cut
Finds its way
Searches for trees
Differentiates
among objects

Physical & cognitive work zone
Understands how and when to use tools
Knows how to move around
Understands how and when to cut
Performs all actions intelligently
Knows where and how to transport
Performs work safely and efficiently

Physical work zone
Has physical strength
Has the power to do work
Is equipped with hammers, chisels, axes and saws
Can transport
Can move

Cognitive capability — High / Low
Physical capability — Low / High

"Once we have done that we can develop a plan to see how to move the non-autonomous digital and physical robots upwards."

That is when the discussion changed from "what are we doing" to how to make it happen.

The rebel beavers had moved downstream and could be seen working to build a dam. Their project had a rough start as Caesar decided to first establish a multi-layered bureaucracy and a reporting system. Roles were detailed to the extreme. Beavers were instructed to strictly follow the line of command. Asking questions was prohibited as part of the policy. Engineers and scientists were asked to focus on research and development and were not allowed to attend the strategy session. Strategy-setting and development was left exclusively in the hands of the Governing and Consultant beavers. Many leaders were picked, and titles were awarded. A clear line of demarcation was drawn by titles, departments, functions, line of authority, ranks and role. Jealousies and internal politics developed quickly. Fiefdoms were established, and turfs defended. In the rush to get results, two teams were hastily sent deep into the forest. While one team returned unharmed, the other team was not that lucky. It was attacked by a pack of hungry wolves. The team members lost their lives long before the winter arrived.

Pure-Play Leadership Lessons

Lesson 17: Prepare your organizations for change. As companies enter the cognitive revolution, organizational readiness is a major issue. Begin by incorporating cognitive-revolution competitive dynamics in your strategies.

Lesson 18: Focus on education. Educate your employees on how to compete in the cognitive era and how to build a sustainable competitive advantage. Plan for the long haul, but start with practical, high-priority projects.

Lesson 19: Be inclusive. Strategic outlook that incorporates cognitive competition must include all functions. Marketing, Operations, Human Resources, Finance, Supply Chain, Legal, Audit, Board Governance –

all functions are changing. An integrated strategy to create a cognitively competitive company requires building a cross-functional team and developing an integrated vision.

Lesson 20: Perform PC-Square exercises constantly. First list your existing process capabilities in terms of non-autonomous software and non-autonomous robots. Then place them on the PC-Square chart. Then define a path to move them upwards by asking the following two questions: (1) What can machines learn about humans and other machines that can be improved by moving software and robots upwards along the cognitive axis? (2) What work can machines perform that can be improved by moving software and robots upwards along the cognitive axis?

Lesson 21: Inspire commitment. Inspire teams to commit to perform such that they find intrinsic motivation to succeed. Make it a shared glory.

6

COGNITIVE CAPABILITIES

"That is a great model," Beaver Leader said to Sarah, then asked, "Can you help us understand what are cognitive capabilities, and how do we move upwards and northeastwards?"

"Sure, Leader. Actually, there is an entire framework," Sarah replied. "We need to think of it as a five-step process: Sense, Analyze, Decide, Act and Learn. As our consultant friend would say, we can have an acronym—SADAL®—pronounced as *saddle*." Sarah looked in the direction where the Consultants were sitting, smiled, and then continued "SADAL® framework means that each intelligent artifact has some level of these elements of Sense, Analyze, Decide, Act and Learn." She then wrote the following on the wall:

Sense   Analyze   Decide   Act   Learn

Sense: A bot uses sensors to receive information from its environment. It can receive data from Vision, Audio, Temperature, Motion and many other types of sensors.

Analyze: It organizes and analyzes the data received via sensors and then performs various analysis.

Decision: It makes decisions based upon the data and its goal structure.

Act: Based upon the decisions made, it acts upon those decisions.

Learn: It evaluates its decisions and actions to determine whether it is coming closer to its goal or drifting away. In other words, it learns from the consequences of its actions and gets better with every iteration.

"Every process performed by the Beaver Bot would need to be detailed for SADAL®," Sarah said. "In other words, we would need to clearly define what will be sensed, what analysis will be made, what decisions will be required, what actions will be taken, and what learning needs to take place. Then we would determine what sensors, analytical tools, decision tools, electromechanical devices, and learning algorithms need to be deployed."

The beavers realized that this was new knowledge for them. They all paid a lot of attention to the details. The rest of the day was spent trying to understand various manifestations of the PC-Square and the SADAL® model for the Beaver Bot project. For example, the beavers took a single process of cutting down a tree and subdivided it into sub-processes such as: (1) determining which tree to cut; (2) understanding the best position to begin the cut; (3) using the best tool; (4) determining the exact force of the tool needed; (5) estimating time it would take to cut; (6) knowing when the tree would fall and in which direction; and (7) moving out of the way of the falling tree.

For each one of these sub-processes, the team established the SADAL® requirements. For example, for determining the position to begin the cut, the bot would need sensors that determine the height, width, density and type of tree. It would then need to organize and analyze the data obtained from the sensors. The analysis will reveal a list of best points to begin the cut. Then, based upon the analysis, it will decide to launch the cut. Its action will be determined by the goal of the sub-process. Once the decision is made on what to do, it will proceed to the act of cutting. It will then have the results and will figure out if it succeeded, and the results were as expected or if it failed. This feedback loop will create learning, and the bot will readjust and realign its analysis, decision making and actions.

"Learning is the key part of intelligence," Sarah explained. "It requires a lot of patience to teach a bot. It's like teaching a baby beaver. Slowly the machine learns to think and perform actions."

At the end of the day Beaver Leader stood up and added the following lessons on the side cave wall:

- Start by understanding the PC-Square Capability Map. This implies that intelligent artifacts need two sets of capabilities—Cognitive Software and Cognitive Robotic.
- Go through process by process and understand which process can be enhanced through electro-mechanical, cognitive, or combined PC-Square intervention. Determine the improvement value of each process.
- Apply the SADAL® framework to each process. This implies that we need to determine "what and how" of sensors, analytical, decision-making, action and learning capabilities will be for the artifact you are building.

A lot was achieved that day. The beavers were excited about the project they had undertaken. With the first meeting concluded, the beavers looked forward to the next day.

The following day, the beavers showed up when it was still dark. They are nocturnal creatures and can go on during the night, but Leader had imposed certain discipline on the team—primarily to make sure to avoid burnouts.

"Today, we will start our beaver bot building process," Beaver Leader said.

"Leader, before we start, I have one question," A Producer member said. "What exactly is learning? I mean I understand how we, the beavers, learn, but how exactly does a bot learn?"

"Great question," Beaver Leader pointed to Sarah and asked, "Do you want to answer the question?"

"Sure, Leader. Well, think of learning as algorithms. We have many algorithms that we use to teach machines. For example, we can use math to find trends in data. That means if we observe a relationship between data, we can identify the trend and then predict the values of some variable. Think of it as teaching the algorithm on how to predict. You provide the input data and sample output data. It is known as labeling the data. Since you know what the right answers are for a given input, you teach the algorithm by providing the right answers. Slowly, your algorithm learns to observe the trend. It's all math."

"Can you give an example?" Producer said.

"Sure, think of a bot trying to determine how much power it should use when it encounters different amounts of snow. Thus, the snowfall measured in inches—known as features in machine learning—could be used to predict how much power would be needed to tread through the woods. This is known as Regression." Sarah showed the following diagram.

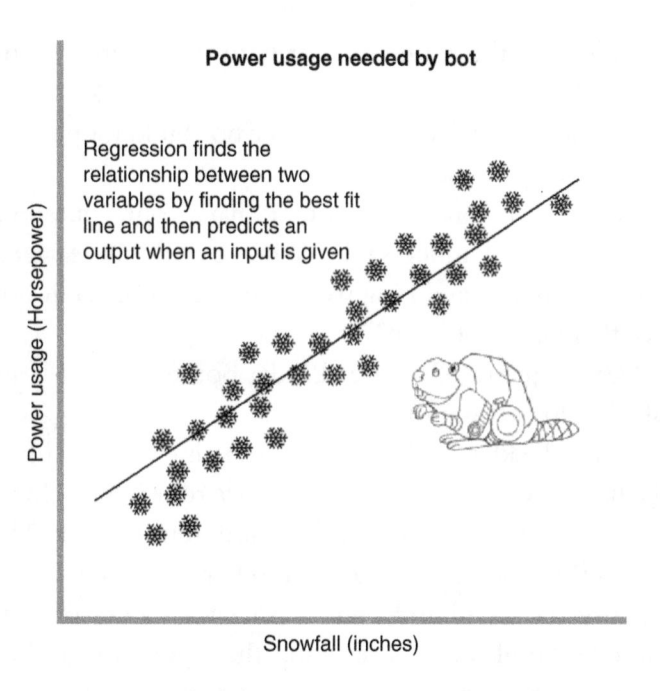

Power usage needed by bot

Regression finds the relationship between two variables by finding the best fit line and then predicts an output when an input is given

Power usage (Horsepower)

Snowfall (inches)

Then she continued. "Another way for a bot to learn is to teach it how to classify things. This is known as Classification. Based upon some features, it distinguishes between different things and, when one thing is given as an input, it can now predict which one it is. For example, trees look different than buffalos and if feature data are provided, an algorithm can classify things with leaves (upper part green) and trunks (one leg) as trees, and things with three or four legs and non-green upper part as buffalos. You can give bot the sample output data about certain features of what you are trying to classify, and then it learns to do that on its own. Learning when sample input and sample output are given is known as Supervised Learning. Both Regression and Classification are Supervised Learning models since in both methods, input and output data are provided."

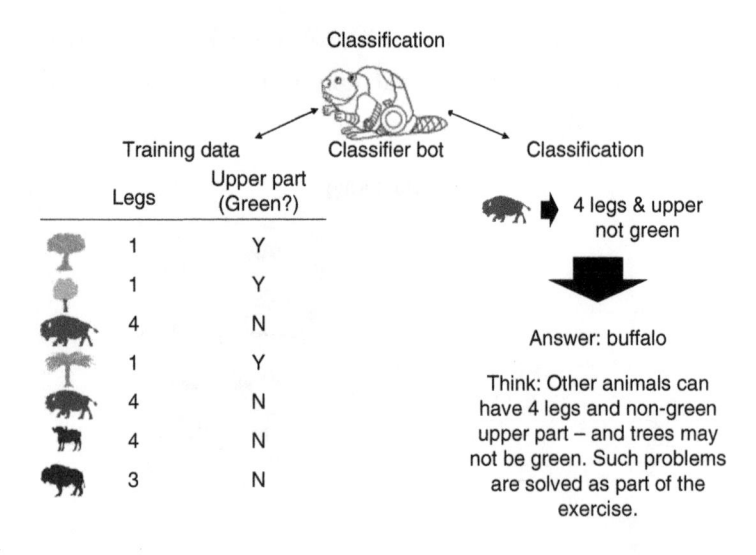

Classification

Classifier bot

Training data

	Legs	Upper part (Green?)
	1	Y
	1	Y
	4	N
	1	Y
	4	N
	4	N
	3	N

Classification

4 legs & upper not green

Answer: buffalo

Think: Other animals can have 4 legs and non-green upper part – and trees may not be green. Such problems are solved as part of the exercise.

"Is there anything that is unsupervised learning?" an Engineer beaver inquired.

"Actually, yes!" Sarah answered. "Learning can also be unsupervised. For example, you can ask an algorithm to differentiate between elks, rabbits and buffalos. It can use the feature "weight" to classify the three. Observe that in this case you don't even need to provide the output sample data. For example, if you take a large sample of buffalos, elks, and rabbits—and plot their weight on a graph, clusters will develop which will place buffalos in one group, elks in another group, and rabbits in a separate group. Now, you didn't even need the output data to teach the algorithm. It observed that the three entities were different based upon the pattern that emerged from the 'weight' feature it was analyzing. In terms of learning, once it has discovered the cluster patterns, as new input is given the algorithm will classify it as part of one of the clusters. If a rabbit comes and the bot knows its weight, it would estimate it is a rabbit and not a buffalo. This is known as Unsupervised Learning and the method used was Clustering."

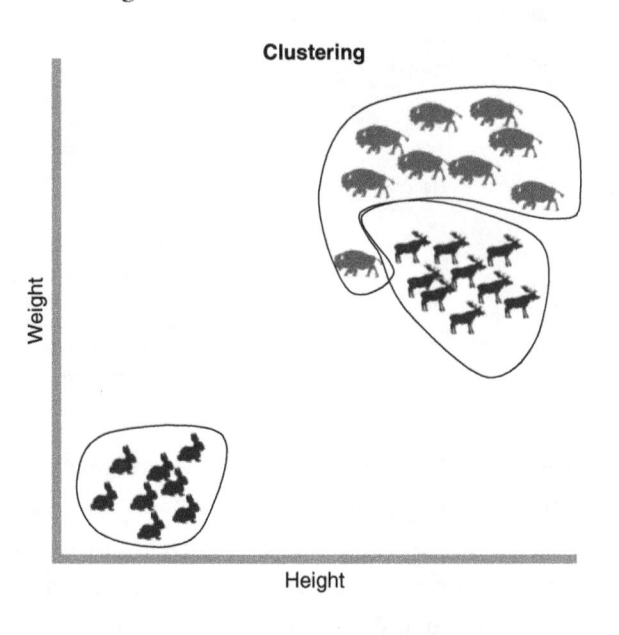

Clustering

Sarah continued. "Then, we also have models that emulate how beaver people's brains work, and they copy the functioning of the brain. That is known as a neural network. In artificial neural networks, we use a system of interconnected processing elements that work together to solve problems. It attempts to mimic the structure of smart beaver brain."

"Sarah, elks weigh an average six hundred pounds and buffalos are seventeen hundred pounds—what if there is a really fat elk?" asked a Consultant. "Wouldn't it end up as a buffalo? Or a really small buffalo that may show up as an elk?"

"Good question," Sarah responded. "Yes, certainly, there is a problem of false-positives and false-negatives, and one of the things we do is to measure the performance of algorithms by minimizing those."

"Thank you, Sarah for a very comprehensive review," said Beaver Leader. "That was very helpful. As you can see, we would need to transform not only how we work but also our basic ways of approaching work. We need to think in terms of learning machines. Now it is time to begin the actual work of building the bot."

While Beaver Leader's team was making progress and followed a disciplined process, internal fighting erupted in the rebel group. Caesar spent most of his time trying to broker peace among various warring department heads. The food supply was running low, and pressure mounted to accelerate the pace of construction. Caesar became more frustrated and hopeless. Other leaders and department heads were also under a lot of stress. Some became disheartened and accepted the fact that they would not be able be construct a dam. Despite that acknowledgment, they made sure to come to work, if only to show their faces.

Pure-Play Leadership Lessons

Lesson 22: Develop SADAL® analysis. Take each process from the PC-Square analysis and break it down based upon the SADAL® framework. This means analyze each process that is being transformed into cognitive state by asking: What are the requirements for automation? Five requirements will be developed: Sense: what sensors will be needed; Analyze: what analysis will be required by machine; Decide: What is the goal for the machine in accordance with which it will make a decision; Act: What is the action required; and Learn: What learning will be needed by the machine.

Lesson 23: Develop a basic understanding of Machine Learning. Machine Learning can be divided into several sub-areas. Two of those are Supervised and Unsupervised Learning. Supervised Learning includes Regression and Classification. Unsupervised Learning includes Clustering.

Additional Explanation: Both digital and physical machines will become smarter. Human Work Automation will continue on both ends—services and manufacturing. It is important for C-level executives to develop a business-level understanding of Artificial Intelligence and high-level Machine Learning concepts. It is also important to understand that evolutionary dynamics of competition will accelerate as greater intelligence emerges.

THE FINAL STRUGGLE

Later that day, work started, and the beaver people placed their entire effort into the construction of the bot. Some beavers worked on the physical capabilities, others on the cognitive software capabilities and a third team worked on integrating the two. What followed was a mixed success. There were failures, learnings and stress but the beavers managed through it all.

In the next five beaver months, work continued in full beaver swing. Many failures and disappointments happened and were overcome through patience and ingenuity.

One version of the beaver bot fell into the creek and could not get itself up. While beavers love swimming, the primary function of the beaver bot was not to swim. It was to go into the forest, cut down trees and bring them back.

The team created another version, but as soon as it entered the forest it was attacked and destroyed by an angry bear. The team made the next version stronger and faster.

This version tripped on a rock and fell, and its sensors broke. The team improved its balance and created a new version.

The new version could not discriminate between trees and rocks and began cutting a rock, damaging electromechanical components such as its axe and saw.

Yet another bot version cut down a tree but was not fast enough to move out of the way of the falling tree and was crushed.

Beaver Leader and Sarah patiently and calmly led the process and motivated teams to turn every disappointment into a success. Slowly, but surely, the teams made progress and in a matter of five months they were finally able to build a fully functional beaver robot.

Beaver Leader returned to the cave and added:

- Making mistakes is an essential part of learning. The only way to build a good bot is to experiment, learn and persevere.

Then the final version was deployed on a test basis and, when it passed the test, it was fully commissioned. The beavers had a major reason to celebrate this accomplishment—winter was fast approaching—so they decided to postpone the celebration until the following year.

Once deployed, the bot did an amazing job. Within one month it had accumulated a lot of food and brought back so much timber, shrubs, logs and rocks that the beavers were able to construct a dam fast. When they finished, it was already in the late months of the beaver calendar and winter had begun. Soon everything would be covered with snow. But the beavers entered the winter knowing they had plenty of food and that the dam had been reconstructed. The birds flew down south for the winter, conscious that the pond was back and functional. The moose, the elk, the deer, the rabbits and other life-forms would also return in the next season. And the beavers had regained their confidence and credibility.

That was when Beaver Leader took a trip downstream to the rebel colony. He saw their dam construction project was a complete failure. He knew that no rebel beaver would survive the winter. He asked them to return to the original colony. The rebel pack did not think twice about that decision and, all of them, including Caesar, followed Beaver Leader to the safety of the new dam. As families reunited and old misunderstandings were forgotten and forgiven, a new era of prosperity and progress began for the colony.

The Beaver Bot of Yellowstone worked round the clock, and even during the winter months. As cold weather came, a thick crust of ice formed on the water, and snow covered everything. The beavers went under water and then through the internal waterway climbed up into their lodges. There, they rested and chewed on their food reserve, waiting for spring to arrive. No one dared leave the lodge except Beaver Leader, who would occasionally go out only so he could watch the Beaver Bot busily doing the work, unaffected by snow and totally ignorant of its own existence. Beaver Leader smiled and said to himself "be a lodgepole pine, Shorty."

Pure-Play Leadership Lessons

Lesson 24: Understand that developing cognitive capabilities will be a long undertaking that will require a disciplined effort and patience. Mistakes will happen along the way, and they are part of learning. Leaders will have to stay resolute in their commitment and continue to invest in the projects. Most importantly, leaders will need to hire the right talent. Hiring traditional consultants or software companies may not the best approach.

Additional Explanation: In the past, you could create powerful competitive advantage by implementing off-the-shelf configurable solutions. It will be different for the cognitive competition. Unlike the old-style technologies, creating a competitive advantage with cognitive technologies is not something that can be achieved by opening a software package. It requires a lot of planning, experimentation, cross-disciplinary effort, adding new types of organizational talent (e.g., linguists, neuroscientists, cognitive scientists, robotics experts, mathematicians, etc.), and patience. Success will come for those who persevere.

8

CEO REFLECTION

Dennis finished telling the story as the three CEOs listened attentively to every word he said. He then went to his truck for more coffee and snacks as well as some paper and pens.

Henry, Bob and Nancy sat at the picnic table, observing the two beavers busy building their dam and completely ignoring their keen visitors, who had just heard a beaver story.

"Dennis, I must say it was a powerful and very moving story," Bob said.

"This was the best damn story I've ever heard!" Henry shouted and shook his head. "And I don't say that easily— now I believe in the power of getting answers from Yellowstone Park."

"Amazing insights," Nancy said as she leaned back, smiled and gave a thumbs-up gesture. "Totally enjoyed it."

Dennis smiled and thanked them.

The sun had risen higher. Across the creek, a moose was grazing. Farther down, buffalos congregated, idly moving in circles. A hump moved lazily in the tall grass— probably a grizzly bear, feeding on berries. Birds were chirping loudly. Breeze touched the flowers as an eagle dived and chased a crow. A coyote howled somewhere in the distance.

Dennis poured coffee for his guests, saying, "Now I would request each one of you to think about the story and tell me how it applies to your business."

"Let me take a shot," Henry said. "The beavers were living in the industrial and information revolution—as we were. Then the environmental dynamics changed, and they had to acquire capabilities of the cognitive era. For example, in our case we are now developing autonomous cars. We are good at making cars, and we've been making them for decades, but now we must add the cognitive dimension. The Beaver Leader's statement, 'We were good at building dams, and now we must be good at building bots that build good dams,' resonated with me a lot. We can't depend on the technology firms to do that for us—since they are becoming our competitors. We are on our own. That means we must excel at both electromechanical and cognitive dimensions."

Bob openly expressed his feelings. "Can't agree more with Henry. We thought of Amazon as a tech firm, but it is a retailer and a supply-chain company. And it is no longer just online—it now has physical stores. It is in our backyard. We must excel at building our bots, and we sure can't rely on Amazon to give us the technology to sell better."

"What I got out of the story is that we need to make smart machines that make, or help make, smart new drugs for us," Nancy said. "This means we are no longer in the drug-making business—we are really in the business of making machines that make better drugs faster. This may include inventing new molecules or diagnostics or therapies. And that is the greatest transformation of our time.

On the hospital side, we need to aggressively advance to remove inefficiencies and improve patient care through the introduction of AIR technologies."

"Nancy—that is an absolutely astounding insight," Dennis said. "It also provides a segue into what you think is the cognitive competition?"

"For me the cognitive competition trophy belongs to the firm that can have the smarter bots or more intelligent systems," Nancy stated in a matter-of-fact manner. "The game is about intelligence now. In other words, if Henry wants to win he'd have to make cars that are not only better in other traditional aspects but also better in cognitive aspects. For example, which autonomous car will be safer, better, smoother, reliable, understands its customer's needs and navigates and drives responsibly through the streets will be the new winner. This whole new dimension is the basis for new competition. In our case, our ability to discover new drugs faster, provide better care to patients, and enable our clinical staff to do their jobs with the bots will be key to our success. It is no longer about who has more information, it is about who is more intelligent."

"Exactly!" Bob said. "The winners in the retail sector will be the ones who have smarter bots. Thus, intelligence or cognitive abilities are the fundamental basis and drivers of competition now."

"You don't compete on the cognitive side and you will die out," Henry said. "Just like the beavers, we have no choice but to build those capabilities. And it doesn't matter what sector you're in. Now that I think about it, every sector has to change. Finance and banking, food, transportation, logistics—you name it. Heck, even government would need to change."

Dennis nodded and said, "Artificial intelligence and robotics can impact the operational and competitive terrain immensely. They provide the ability to evaluate, assess, decide and act. Cognitive capabilities ease the process of infringement into other industries and redefine the notion of information technology—thus enabling tech firms to enter non-tech domains. They can as easily build a hedge fund bot as they can build an autonomous car technology. The ability to gain experience enhances product development exponentially—meaning that a product that comes into existence first will acquire more experience than the one that comes later—and hence leads to unique competitive advantages that ultimately disrupts the market dynamics permanently."

Dennis placed a diagram in front of the group. It showed the following figure:

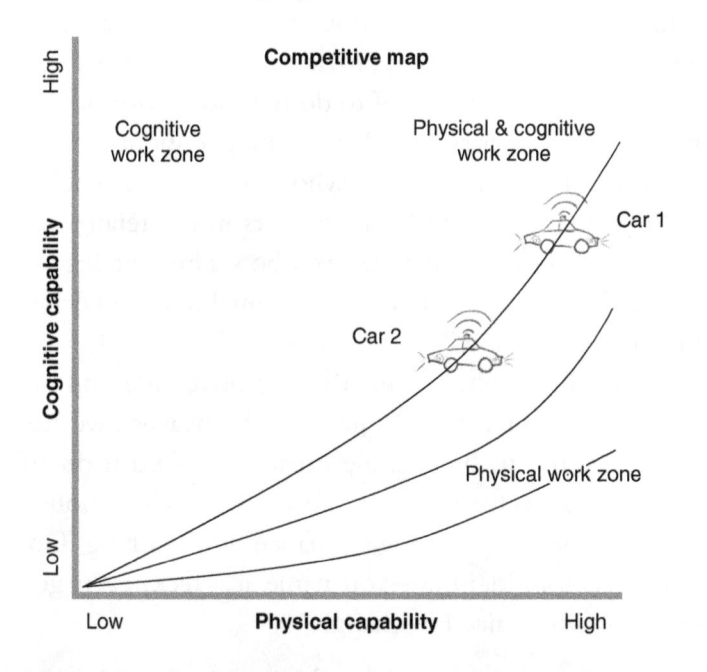

"Since it does better on both cognitive and physical dimensions, Car 1 in this example can provide a greater source of competitive advantage over Car 2," Dennis said. "And the way to determine which car is more advanced in cognitive terms, you use the SADAL® framework to benchmark yourself against other competitors."

Then he asked, "How do you think you can lead and implement such transformations in your firms?"

Pure-Play Leadership Lesson

Lesson 25: Develop a solid understanding of the new competitive dynamic that implies that competitive advantage is now a function of "intelligence" or "cognitive capabilities."

"I liked the approach Beaver Leader took," Henry said. "We need to form teams that are composed of cross-functional members. We need to examine our processes and perform the PC-Square analysis on them. We need to then look at the SADAL® analysis for each process. Based upon that, we can formulate and plan out our transformation."

"We do need executive sponsorship and to have the board behind it," Nancy said, "Just as Beaver Leader placed his full power and vision behind the transformation, we must, too. Also, this will be a major change, so we need to prepare our people for that."

Dennis said, "So, let me now borrow the learnings that Beaver Leader wrote on the wall and make some minor adjustments to them and give you something you can take with you." He gave them each a laminated sheet of paper with the following:

Creating the Future in the Cognitive Era

- Decide on renewal. Make an executive decision to reinvent and redefine yourself.
- Understand that this journey means building dual competencies in both your native-core competencies and tech-based bot building.
- Lead the cultural transformation to create unparalleled innovation.
- Organize a cross-functional team to launch a major effort.
- Start by understanding the PC-Square Capability Map. Intelligent artifacts need upward movement by enhancing Software and Robotics.
- Go through process by process and understand which can be enhanced through upward movement in the PC-Square intervention. Determine the improvement value of each process.
- Apply the SADAL® framework to each process. This implies that we need to determine "what and how" of sensors, analytical, decision-making, action, and learning capabilities will be for the artifact you are building.
- Making mistakes is an essential part of learning. The only way to build a good bot is to experiment, learn, and persevere.
- Understand and have your boards and employees understand that competition is now about "cognitive competition."
- Create an internal measure of cognitive competition map and constantly benchmark yourself against competitors.

Each of the executives studied the page with its title, "Creating the Future in the Cognitive Era."

"And here is the summary of lessons of being a Pure-Play Leader." Dennis passed on the list to them.

Pure-Play Leadership Lessons

Lesson 1: All firms are now tech firms and should be led as such. A cognitive business is a business that derives its competitive advantage via intelligent automation.

Lesson 2: Pure-play leadership is the ability to effectively lead a firm from a traditional to a cognitive business through a systematic and disciplined effort such that the firm expands and leverages its incumbent advantage while simultaneously fostering new cognitive capabilities.

Lesson 3: The traditional barriers to entry are no longer valid. Competition can come from anywhere.

Lesson 4: Authenticity is key to being a pure-play leader. "Fake it till you make it" will not work.

Lesson 5: Pretending to be a tech culture is futile. Employees will see right through it and the traditional turf wars and destructive politics will not end.

Lesson 6: Pure-play leaders recognize that successful pure-play leadership will be the greatest test of their leadership and careers (refer to the definition of pure-play leadership).

Lesson 7: Denial is not an option. The fourth industrial revolution has arrived, and there is no option but to respond. Clear thinking and a calm courageous demeanor will be essential.

Lesson 8: Be decisive. Pure-play leaders are decisive. Once they decide, they are quick to implement.

Lesson 9: Speed of execution is essential. Do not wait. Act fast. Drive results. Pure-play leaders understand that timing is everything.

Lesson 10: Handle relentless pressure. Get used to extremely aggressive deadlines. Learn to deal with the immense pressure. Work becomes constant, and it may feel like nothing exists except work. But that is the only way when extraordinary results are achieved.

Lesson 11: Develop "wow" product and service focus. Pure-play leaders have no time for petty politics. Their leadership is authentic and focused on only one thing: improving the future with a "wow" product or service that truly add value for consumers.

Lesson 12: The cool factor. Pure-play leaders love to pursue the challenge of delivering "wow" products and services. It is not their persona, but the integrated ecosystem that becomes cool. The products and services, processes, people, culture, brands—everything transforms into cool.

Lesson 13: Destroy elitism. Pure-play leaders do not create silos or a caste system between those who are "strategic" people and those who are not.

Lesson 14: Truth is power. Rational and data-driven decision making is key. Ambition is always nurtured and guided by rationality and data-driven search for truth.

Lesson 15: All held accountable by all. Pure-play leaders make sure that systems are implemented that hold all accountable by all. Authority is not top-down but emerges through a collective commitment to accomplish great things.

Lesson 16: Dual Leadership. Implies leaders identify the core competence of their firm and then extrapolate it to the tech level. For example, we are good in making drugs, and now we must become good in making technology that discovers and makes new medicines.

Lesson 17: Prepare your organizations for change. As companies enter the cognitive revolution, organizational readiness is a major issue. Begin by incorporating cognitive-revolution competitive dynamics in your strategies.

Lesson 18: Focus on education. Educate your employees on how to compete in the cognitive era and how to build a sustainable competitive advantage. Plan for the long haul, but start with practical, high-priority projects.

Lesson 19: Be inclusive. Strategic outlook that incorporates cognitive competition must include all functions: Marketing, Operations, Human Resources, Finance, Supply Chain, Legal, Audit, Board Governance—all functions are changing. An integrated strategy to create a cognitively competitive company requires building a cross-functional team and developing an integrated vision.

Lesson 20: Perform PC-Square exercises constantly. First list your existing process capabilities in terms of non-autonomous software and non-autonomous robots. Then place them on the PC-Square chart. Then define a path to move them upwards by asking the following two questions: (1) What can machines learn about humans and other machines that can be improved by moving software and robots upwards along the cognitive axis? (2) What work can machines perform that can be improved by moving software and robots upwards along the cognitive axis?

Lesson 21: Inspire commitment. Inspire teams to commit to perform such that they find intrinsic motivation to succeed. Make it a shared glory.

Lesson 22: Develop SADAL® analysis. Take each process from the PC-Square analysis and break it down based upon the SADAL® framework. This means analyze each process that is being transformed into a cognitive state by asking what will be the requirements for automation. Five requirements will be developed: Sense: What sensors will be needed; Analyze: What analysis will be required by machine; Decide: What is the goal for the machine in accordance with which it will make decisions; Act: What is the action required; and Learn: What learning will be needed by the machine.

Lesson 23: Develop the basic understanding of Machine Learning. Machine Learning can be divided into several sub-areas. Two of those are Supervised and Unsupervised Learning. Supervised learning includes Regression and Classification. Unsupervised Learning includes Clustering.

Lesson 24: Understand that developing cognitive capabilities will be a long undertaking that will require a disciplined effort and patience. Mistakes will happen along the way and they are part of learning.

Lesson 25: Develop a solid understanding of the new competitive dynamic that implies that competitive advantage is now a function of "intelligence" or "cognitive capabilities."

"Dennis this was so worth it," Henry said. "I am so happy I attended this conference."

"I hope you don't mind me asking what's your background," Bob asked Dennis.

"Well, I built and sold a tech company and made some good money. Then, I decided to retire and become a guide and facilitator to teach others how to manage innovation. I spend summer months here, fall months in the Grand Canyon, and then go to Aspen during the winter months. Between hiking, skiing and coaching the days go by fast."

"Well, we are glad you do that Dennis. It helped us a lot," Henry said, as Bob and Nancy nodded in agreement.

"Thanks. So here is what I noticed. I realized that corporate executives of large firms are so busy in their day-to-day thinking, so influenced by old-school strategy consultants, and so entrenched that they don't realize when real major change of events happen. That is why small and nimble innovative firms can adapt rapidly and become leaders. But, today, your threat is not just from small firms. It is from the 'culture of innovation' and multidisciplinary expertise that large tech firms have acquired.

"Think of it this way," Dennis continued, "you know that innovation is one of your greatest drivers of value. It is innovation that determines the competitive dynamics. You know that, on the one hand, you need to encourage and orchestrate a culture that encourages innovation. On the other hand, you also know that in order to establish a competitive advantage you need to develop a core competence in your traditional domain. It would be retail for you, Bob, health care for you, Nancy, and automotive for you, Henry. But that is not enough. Today, you need to have multidimensional competence that goes above and beyond your native competency sector. You need dual competencies. Which means, you need to have a powerful culture of innovation that drives innovation—not just in your traditional areas, but also in the technology domains."

Dennis paused before saying, "And that's where you'd need to figure out how you will become the lodgepole pine."

QUESTIONS FOR REVIEW

Chapters 1 and 2

What are the most profound strategic and competitive challenges facing your firm?

What are the direct threats to your business from emerging artificial intelligence and robotics?

What impact would these threats have on your business?

Chapter 3

In what areas can you build "intelligence" based on your current competitive advantage?

In what ways would "intelligence" create a competitive advantage in your industry?

Which firms should serve as benchmarks for excellence in "intelligence"?

Chapter 4

In what areas can you automate work in your firm?

In what areas can you apply Robotic Process Automation?

What is your PC-Square analysis for each major process in your firm?

Which projects are directly related to your competitive advantage? How can you prioritize them?

What resources and support do you need to execute identified projects successfully?

What is your investment path? What is your return on investment on intelligent transformation?

Chapter 5

What is the state of existing capabilities of your firm to compete in the "intelligent" economy?

In what areas you need help?

What timelines do you need to consider?

What standards do you need to follow?

What social, legal and regulatory considerations do you need to consider?

Chapter 6

What specific learning and training is needed to launch your transformation to an intelligent firm?

What resources are needed to support this effort?

What timelines would work best for your firm?

Chapter 7

What are the failure points?

What are your biggest project risks?

What defines success?

QUESTIONS FOR DEEPER INSIGHTS

What do artificial intelligence (AI) and robotic process automation (RPA) mean for your firm?

How do AI and RPA align with your vision, mission and goals?

What is the role of artificial intelligence and robotic process automation in your industry?

How does it impact processes and competitive advantage?

Do you have an AI- and RPA-centric business plan or strategic plan?

What changes need to take place in key organizational functions such as Operations, Marketing, Finance, IT and Human Resources among others?

How do you think leadership will change with AI and RPA?

How do you think management will change with AI/RPA?

What are the ethical issues of AI/RPA?

How do you think AI/RPA should be governed?

ABOUT THE AUTHORS

Al (A.I.) Naqvi has pioneered the field of Enterprise Artificial Intelligence. He developed the first and most comprehensive body of knowledge (and courses) for AI in corporate strategy, AI in finance, AI in marketing, AI in HR, AI in competitive intelligence, and AI in supply chain management. The courses developed by Naqvi are now offered by George Mason University. He is the editor of the *Journal of Artificial Intelligence in Business, Policy, and Economy*. He is a leading expert in transforming companies from the "e" to the "ai" era and specializes in total and integrated business transformation by using artificial intelligence. Naqvi's work has been recognized by world's leading professional societies, universities and companies. Over 300 companies have benefited from his research. He is widely published in both academic and practitioner publications. Naqvi's professional research interests are broad, and include artificial intelligence, deep learning applied AI, robotic process automation, complex adaptive systems, cognitive organizations and leadership, and strategic cognitive transformation. He teaches several classes on Applied Artificial Intelligence, Deep Learning, RPA, and Cognitive Transformation at the American Institute of Artificial Intelligence. Naqvi is passionate about teaching people about the potential and practical applications of artificial intelligence. He calls it reskilling and re-intellectualization of the workforce. He has designed several products using Deep Neural Networks. Known for making artificial intelligence fun and easy to understand, Naqvi has appeared in various conferences and shows all over the world. He lives in the greater Washington, DC, area.

J. Mark Munoz is a tenured full professor of management and international business at Millikin University in Illinois, and a former visiting fellow at the Kennedy School of Government at Harvard University. He is the recipient of several awards, including four Best Research Paper awards, a literary award, an International Book Award, and the ACBSP Teaching Excellence Award among others. Aside from top-tier journal publications, he has authored/edited/coedited 18 books, including *Land of My Birth, Winning across Borders, A Salesman in Asia, International Social Entrepreneurship, Handbook on the Geopolitics of Business, Advances in Geoeconomics and Global Business Intelligence.* As chairman / CEO of the international management consulting fi rm Munoz and Associates International, he directs consulting projects worldwide in the areas of strategy formulation, business development and international finance.

PART TWO OF THE BEAVER STORY

As Beaver Bots became smarter and did even more work, the beavers became lazy and lost their work ethic. Quarrels developed over what was the role of beavers in the new era. Beaver Bots also became more autonomous and began cutting trees faster than they could grow back. This began impacting the forest

Beaver Leader knew that he had a new problem on his hands. This time, the problem was how to manage and govern the Beaver Bots.

He was ready to take a trip to his favorite geyser, when—

Read the rest in the upcoming book: *Beaver Bots Invade the Grand Canyon: Managing and Governing Artificial Intelligence.*